I Got You

BY
FAYE THOMPSON

I Got You

Copyright © 2023: Faye Thompson

All rights reserved. No part of this publication may be produced, distributed, or transmitted in any form or by any means, including photocopying, recording, or other electronic or mechanical methods, without the prior written permission of the publisher, except in the case of brief quotations embodied in critical reviews and certain other non-commercial uses permitted by copyright law.

First Printed in United Kingdom 2023

Published by Conscious Dreams Publishing
www.consciousdreamspublishing.com

Edited by Daniella Blechner and Elise Abram

Book Design (interior) Ces Rosanna Price
Typesetter Amit Dey

ISBN: 978-1-915522-43-6

Dedication

I dedicate this book firstly to my biggest inspirations, my supporters, my two blessings Nika and Kedar-Re and to all those who have supported me on this journey called life.

We are all spiritual beings inhabiting a temporary body, weaving our way through it.

You know who you are.

I am grateful. I thank you.

Blessed love.

Table of Contents

Introduction vii
Chapter 1: Staying Positive Through Affirmations 1
Chapter 2: Freedom of Choice............................9
Chapter 3: Self-love.................................... 17
Chapter 4: Be Intentional................................ 29
Chapter 5: Build and Support 39
Chapter 6: Commitment 45
Chapter 7: Love and Intimacy 53
Chapter 8: Respect...................................... 63
Chapter 9: Forgiveness 71
Chapter 10: Gratitude 79
Chapter 11: Reliability 89
Chapter 12: Love 97
Chapter 13: Honesty 107
Chapter 14: Communication............................ 113
Chapter 15: Trust...................................... 127
Chapter 16: The Languages of Love 133
Glossary of Words and Terms.......................... 159
About the Author 163
Acknowledgments..................................... 165

Introduction

'She's shy', 'Faye lacks confidence', 'she never answers questions in class, but her written work is good.'

These were the words swimming around my mind from the moment I heard them during my early childhood and well into my adulthood. These words lived and breathed rent-free in my mind for decades. Words are powerful. They can make or break us. Now, I refuse to let these words define me. I'm sure you've heard words throughout your life that have stuck with you, too.

It took years to realise that these comments were stuck in my subconscious mind. This was more damaging than anyone could ever realise.

I'm a 70's baby so I grew up in an era where sayings like, 'little children should be seen and not heard' and worst of all, 'only speak when you're spoken to' were commonly used and believed. In hindsight, I can see now how sayings such as these shaped my sense of self and played a part in me losing my voice.

My motive behind writing this book was because I had been told so many times that I was 'shy' and 'reserved'. This reserved demeanour and shyness affected my ability to communicate effectively with others and this leaked into my relationships. I would repeatedly find myself settling for less, or unable to speak up when it was necessary. On the rare occasions I spoke up, it would often be from a place of blame or anger that someone or something had not lived up to my expectations. We've all been there. Perhaps you, too, have faced much disappointment. Having experienced a lot of rejection in my life, I found it hard to accept being loved and treated well. When I was, I'd often choose to leave the situation, believing I was not able to meet their needs.

In my late teens, I found myself in a very abusive relationship and an unforgettable situation. The shame and anger I felt prevented me from seeking counselling and getting the healing I desperately needed. I lacked self-awareness and neglected my needs. I'd brushed my authentic emotions of anger, shame and grief under the carpet and soldiered on. Aren't we often told that in society? 'Keep Calm and Carry on?'

I kept my chin up and plastered a smile on my face. I didn't realise that my internal, subconscious mind was taking a battering or that my self-esteem and self-worth were in hiding. I became more passive in relationships, often due to fear of aggressive behaviour or negative criticism.

This book is to help you navigate a way to embrace happier and healthier relationships. Having experienced unhealthy relationships and not speaking up for myself, I know how essential it is for both parties to communicate effectively. If we could all be a little more kind, considerate, and compassionate towards each other, especially the people we say we love, wouldn't we all have better relationships and healthy interactions? The aim of this book is to offer you new ways to introduce thoughtful communicated leading to more fulfilling and enriching relationships.

Historically, I attracted relationships that became a one-way street. These relationships lasted way too long for the wrong reasons. I became passive in speaking my truth and I felt as though my needs didn't matter. I'd bury my feelings for so long that when I did finally speak up, my words were never received with the compassion or understanding I needed. Instead, my words and actions were construed as nagging, moaning, or being needy. This book will allow you to learn how to communicate your feelings in a compassionate and assertive way. It's important to have your feelings acknowledged and validated. You matter.

Mistakes can be our greatest teacher. The mistakes and poor choices I have made inspired me to write this book. 'I Got You' is a light-hearted but thoughtful interactive book that contains quotes, positive affirmations, reflections and questions to ask yourself. It might be too much to say it's a survival guide, but at least it's a thought-provoking, honest look at the ways we communicate with each other.

I wrote this book because if you struggle to speak up for yourself, I want you to know your voice is important. I hope that through this book, you will gain some effective tools to help you ask for what you need and begin to have open and honest conversations with yourself. I know how it feels to hold everything in and never show our feelings. Sometimes one person can't do it all. It's kind to be supportive, but don't forget yourself.

We all need a little help in our lives..

Bestow support and gratefully receive.

Faye x

Chapter 1

Staying Positive Through Affirmations

In this book, we will use affirmations to help refocus the mindset to a more positive state. Positive affirmations are declarations that help us overcome unhelpful mindsets or prevent us from sabotaging ourselves. They are statements that reinforce positive ideas and thoughts about ourselves, others, and the world we experience. They are best used in a repetitious way, so you may wish to do this every morning or evening for 30 days.

Positive alignment with affirmations

At the end of each section, you will find a list of positive affirmations. You can either read them in your head or read them out loud whenever you feel the need to reaffirm the statement. You can use these affirmations whenever you desire and at any point in time in your life. You can also write some of your own, too! Positive affirmations help us align ourselves with positive thoughts, feelings, and actions, and therefore, experience positive outcomes in our lives.

When we wallow in places of negative self-talk or low energy, we attract more negative situations. Equally, if we come from mindsets of positivity, we attract more energy to create astonishing things.

Negativity can ruin relationships

Sometimes in relationships, we only see the flaws in those we once claimed to love so much. One day they're the perfect partner, then suddenly, everything they say or do gets on our nerves!

We could then ask ourselves if perhaps they were always like that or if they dropped their mask. What has happened? Why have we become so unaligned? What has changed, when, and why?

Did you stop taking them out? Did you forget to treat them like a king or queen? Did you stop appreciating each other? Did you stop giving? Did you stop going out together? Did you just get bored with the monotony of not moving forward? Was it the toothpaste lid that was left off for the millionth time, or the toilet seat lid up or down saga?

Did you allow your life to be taken over by the children, so much so that you forgot that a fun and saucy love life was a part of your relationship? You know these things don't have to stop when you have a child or children. Even old age shouldn't make it go downhill and end.

Perhaps you stopped communicating kindly, called each other names, or behaved in a way that is unacceptable.

Please note, there is never an excuse for domestic abuse whether it's emotional, physical or financial. If you are in an abusive relationship, please seek help immediately because no amount of self-development on your side will change the actions of another.

Whatever the reason is, do you both want to give up? Do you tolerate each other? Do you take a good look at the challenges, work through the issues, possibly forgive, and press the reset button?

Increasingly, people find that this can be hard to do, so perhaps you should accept the issue that happened, speak about it, deal with it, and agree there is no need to bring it back up again so you can move on. The choice is yours; you know what you feel.

At the end of the day, we all have flaws, but we can also be what I call flawsome! Accept your flaws and be awesome, anyway! Don't let your flaws hold you back. Be flawsome!

Using positive affirmations to get back on track

Sometimes, we may become so complacent in our relationships that we forget the positive attributes our partners bring to the table or even the positive qualities of our relationships. Sometimes, we may even feel a little insecure about ourselves, and our negative self-talk can be what affects the relationship. You could try giving yourself the challenge of creating your own positive affirmations.

Affirmations are used to make positive transformations in your life. Once you get started, you will begin to feel the difference. Just like your muscles, when you start to exercise, you feel achy or want to give up, but you realise it is for your greater good and peace of mind.

Remember, you had a why and a purpose for the shift. Give yourself a fixed time each day to repeat your affirmations, if that helps with consistency. If you make this a regular practise, you'll see the difference as you begin to transform into a better you.

Examples

Here are some examples of affirmations you could use for yourself and your relationship.

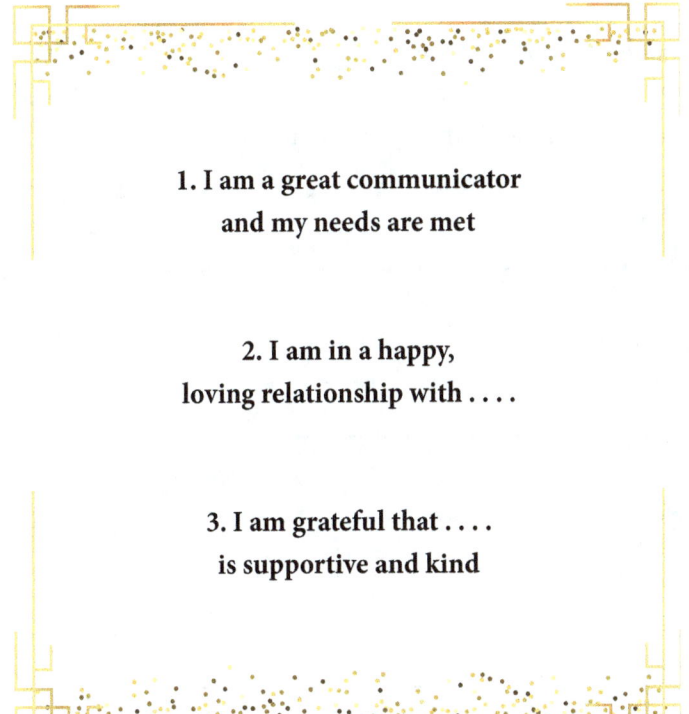

1. I am a great communicator
and my needs are met

2. I am in a happy,
loving relationship with . . . .

3. I am grateful that . . . .
is supportive and kind

My Positive Affirmations

Here's your challenge for today:
Create seven of your own positive personal relationship affirmations, using 'I am…' positive statements only.

1. _____
   _____
   _____
   _____

2. _____
   _____
   _____
   _____

3. _____
   _____
   _____

4. _____
_____
_____
_____

5. _____
_____
_____
_____

6. _____
_____
_____
_____

7. _____
_____
_____
_____

Chapter 2

Freedom of Choice

> *'You must love in such a way that the person you love feels free.'*
>
> —Thich Nhat Hanh

Finding an equilibrium

In loving relationships, we need to find appropriate equilibriums of personal freedom and dedication. When two people in a partnership can be together in a way that respects the other's personal space and also express unambiguous commitment, then both parties can relax and be who they are.

Everyone has the right to make a choice. Occasionally, we make choices on a whim or after having a bad day. Research shows that you make better choices in the morning or when you're not hungry or angry.

It is better to make an informed choice than to live with regrets. Every now and again, though, it's worth the risk. Well-informed choices help you gain clarity over a situation. Clarity clears the cloudiness from any decision you're about to make, and you can come to your own conclusions.

Occasionally, you may make a choice and realise halfway through that you have changed your mind. This might be because your original thought no longer serves you. The idea may have stunted its progress in your life, leaving you wondering what happened.

From time to time, we don't always make the so-called 'right decision', but if I have learnt one thing, it's that 'if it makes you happy, do it; if it doesn't, then don't.'

Experience dictates choice

We use our experiences—or lack thereof—when we choose. We can get to the point where we feel like we are at a dead-end road. Our minds can become turbulent, overthink, and anxiety can set in. You're at a fork in the road, and what lies ahead will shape your future for the next day, week, month, or years to come.

So, at this point, I invite you to choose to change a situation, idea, or perspective, or choose to accept a situation for what it is and leave the situation. These are simple solutions to some of our problems. Whatever you decide, ensure it leaves you a better-off, kinder, and happier person.

We all have choices to make. Your attitude to life is a choice, and the people you choose to surround yourself with are a reflection of you. Are you kind-hearted, respectful, grateful, compassionate, and/or optimistic? Think about the vibes you give out. Your heart's magnetic energy field gives out the most energy, and it can be felt by others from at least three feet away, that's 60-times more amplitude than the electrical activity generated by the brain. (HearthMath Institute)

Your choices, poor choices, good choices, or even no choice is still a choice. Whatever you choose, think about its significance prudently. Who do you let into your circle? Are they good influences on you? What is their purpose on your journey? Are they positive thinkers or dramatic all the time? Are they kind and considerate? Are they dependable even when it's not a time of need? Do they only contact you when they need something?

So, it seems everyone has freedom of choice, and I have noticed, for the most part, there's a set of people that will do anything for others. Equally, I have seen that there is a set of people who do things that only please themselves. I am not saying either is right or wrong because that's a perception, but someone appears to come out being disappointed.

There are many types of people in the world, however, let's think about two basic personality traits 'the givers and the takers'.

Givers

Givers are the people that will always dip into their own well and support others. They think about their needs as well as the other person's needs. Examples of this act of giving could be that they give the last fiver from their pocket even if it means them going without; they give gifts even when they know they don't really have it to give or they help people that wouldn't necessarily give back if they needed the same support.

Takers

Takers are people that can be self-absorbed and put their own needs and interests ahead of others' needs majority of the time. Their actions almost always benefit themselves even if someone is disadvantaged by their actions and find themselves always taking with little reciprocity.

Balanced

Balanced people can be those who know when to give and when to receive. They are happy with being able to give and are open to receiving. They have the mindset of thinking before they act. They understand they have primary priorities and honour them unselfishly. Balanced people have an understanding that you have to take one day at a time and it's not possible to always do and be everything all the time. When you are balanced and have a balanced person around you, the chances are you will achieve successful outcomes because you can do things together for the greatest good.

Reflections

Question Time: Are you a giver or a taker?

There are both givers and takers in this world. Review the text above to summarise the personality traits of givers and takers:

Givers: _____
_____
_____
_____
_____

Takers: _____
_____
_____
_____
_____

Which one are you?

I am a (circle one):

> **giver**   **taker**   **balanced**

Take an honest look at your personality by answering the following questions:

Have the circumstances in which you have been in or dissatisfactions you've endured made you feel differently towards someone you love, and did you change as a result?

_____

_____

_____

_____

_____

_____

_____

What was the short- or long-term impact of the choice(s) you made?

Are you a giver or a taker? How does (or did) this serve its purpose in your life?

Do you think it's possible to balance your lifestyle?

If yes, how will you do this? If no, why not?

1. _____
   _____
   _____
   _____
   _____

2. _____
   _____
   _____
   _____
   _____

3. _____
   _____
   _____
   _____
   _____

Chapter 3

Self Love

'Loving oneself isn't hard when you understand who and what yourself is. It has nothing to do with the shape of your face, the size of your eyes, the length of your hair or the quality of your clothes. It's so beyond all those things, and it's what gives life to everything about you. Your own self is such a treasure.'

—*Phylicia Rashad*

Self-validation

There are some days you may not feel like the best version of yourself, but regardless of that, find peace in knowing you're not the only one.

Though we often wait for validation or reassurance from others, you are important and valuable to yourself. Be mindful that there are many ways to express love and everyone's love language is different. Remember, even if people haven't verbally expressed their love, it doesn't mean they haven't thought it or said it out loud to someone else. Maybe it just takes a lot for them to give words of affirmation or compliments. I would say to be yourself. If you like to give compliments, then that's who you are, and you should be your authentic self. You should have the courage to let your thoughts be known.

When you do, give a compliment, make sure you are doing it from your heart and not because you want affection or a compliment in return. Some people don't give direct, meaningful compliments. They may show their love in other ways, such as through their actions and acts of service. Learn how your partner shows their love and remember it's okay if it's different from the way you do. All relationships take work and it's an act of self-love to express to the person you're with how you like to receive love. Self-validation is the feeling of having recognised, confirmed, or established one's own worthiness or legitimacy (Merrian Webster). Speaking your truth and loving yourself enough to express your needs is essential to this.

Practice self-love and self-care

Some time ago, after what felt like a few apparently failed attempts at relationships, I had the expectation that I was supposed to receive flowers from a person who loved me.

I remember that, at the start of 2016, I started buying myself flowers every week. I love flowers. I really love their beauty and appreciate the intricacy of their making, but for some reason, I had the mindset that someone should buy them for me. I had been in a few relationships where I'd received none whatsoever or received them under duress (LOL—I won't go into that one!).

One New Year, in 2016, I decided that if I wanted flowers, I wouldbuy them myself. Interestingly, I received a few bunches of flowers that year that I hadn't expected at all, and I was truly grateful for the reasons I'd received them. Like words of affirmation, our repeated actions and thoughts towards ourselves attract those things on the same vibration. Want flowers? Buy them yourself!

Despite how people treat you, continue self-love and self-care, so your cup generously overflows regardless of whether you need validation from anyone. Certify yourself.

You're worth it, always.

Reminders to Self

Love and support yourself to make it easier
to be loved and supported by others.

Make yourself feel good first.

Learn to love yourself and really reflect
on the amazing things about yourself.

Give to yourself that which you would
consider giving to another.

Inspire others to feel good, too.

Relaxation and being happy should
be your indulgences in life.

Focus and clear your mind of negativity
and get on with a particular task
you can achieve your goals.

Surround yourself with a
positive circle of friends.

Be immersed in adventures and activities
that make you feel joyful.

Relax, be yourself, and surround yourself
with good-hearted people.

Laugh every day. Find something to smile about.

Be happy and strive to be happier.

Even if you feel broken or sad, rise above it.

Know that someone needs you
and loves you deeply.

Work on having joy and happiness
as a priority; it starts within.

Make your dreams a reality.

Keep up your pursuits and passion.

Live in cheerfulness.

Let your mindset be a place of the
overflowing abundance of positive thoughts.

Build a kind, loving, harmonious relationship with
yourself and see what manifests.

Dance like no one's watching!

Fight your fears and worries always.

Don't let them get the best of you.

We all make mistakes; just don't live in them and do a rerun of the moment that has passed. Keep it in the moment. Don't allow mistakes to hold you prisoner. Stay present, acknowledge the insight, wisdom, or lesson from it, and keep it moving forward.

Build on your inner resilience and determination. You are destined for success.

Acknowledge the amazingness of your contribution to the world.

Treat yourself how you would like to be treated.

Reflections

Question Time: Show yourself you care.

Take a moment to think carefully. This doesn't have to be a list of expensive treats—it may be something as simple as taking a walk in nature to gather your thoughts, mindfulness breathing, or taking a day off for mental health.

What do you do to show yourself love or self-care?

1. _____

_____

_____

_____

_____

2. _____

_____

_____

_____

3. _____

_____

_____

_____

_____

_____

4. _____

_____

_____

_____

_____

_____

5. _____

_____

_____

_____

_____

_____

I Got You

6. _____
_____
_____
_____
_____
_____

7. _____
_____
_____
_____
_____
_____

Words of Affirmation

Look in the mirror and repeat with conviction:

I am worthy.

I am abundant.

I am amazing.

I am beautiful/handsome.

I am blessed.

I am capable.

I am determined.

I am enough.

Chapter 4

Be Intentional

'The biggest coward is a man who awakens a woman's love with no intention of loving her.'

—Bob Marley

Be yourself

Be honest, truthful, authentic, and forthcoming about your intentions. Don't pretend to be someone you're not. Eventually, the mask will fall off, and people will think, *Wow, you have changed*. When, in fact, this is probably who you are unless you have changed your circle of friends and the people in that circle do not have a positive influence. Be yourself now, or you will pay for it later.

'I once heard a phrase: every man has a plan.'

—Steve Harvey

Strategise to avoid self-sabotage

Men know exactly who you are going to be in their lives. I don't think I need to go through the options of who you could be to them at this point, as many of us already know. I think that women know, too. We sometimes change our minds because we notice differences in people's initial plans, red flags pop up, and we might then guard our hearts.

There's also the possibility of self-sabotage. When you have been hurt, you start looking out for patterns experienced in the past, this may be a blessing or a hindrance. When you look for negativity, it shows up like the police knocking down your door.

At that point, we may think about how to make an exit plan. However, sometimes, you may feel there is something worth saving, and want to improve the relationship instead. Deep down, only you know what is best for you, but don't ignore the red flags. You cannot turn red into green!

If you're in a relationship and you are done with suggesting date nights in or out, weekends away, or getting away from the monotony in life, if there's no joy in changing the experience you currently both having, would you consider before all else fails that perhaps relationship counselling might be an option for you?

'When you are clear on your intention you take inspired action that's in alignment with your words and truth.'

—Stephanie Zamora

Know when to move on

Sometimes we may find it hard to move on. You've spent years, sometimes decades, building a what you thought was strong foundation only to let it all go. It hurts. Some of us may live in limbo hoping for a glimmer of change. Perhaps the fear of change creates a toxic, fear-based bond with the partner. This unhealthy bond keeps us tied to a relationship that has far passed its expiry date and even though neither partner is happy, both are too afraid to leave and step out into the unknown. Relationships can be complicated. Throw in houses, finances and children, it becomes far more complex than just two people who want to be together. Despite the breakdown of a relationship, some people need to take time to get used to the idea of the potential loss of their partners' presence, so they keep them there because they need financial security, companionship and/or familiarity.

When the relationship is over and it's the end of that season and all avenues of help have been exhausted, it's important to know your limit. Are you really happy holding on? Is this making your partner happy? Sometimes, no matter what is being done to rectify and bring back the spark, usually one half of the couple has mentally and emotionally left the relationship already.

For the other partner, who perhaps thought things were getting better, when a relationship or marriage ends, it may come as a shock or surprise. They may have thought 'this could still work' or 'we should keep trying', but the decision is made when the partner says they are leaving for good!

Sometimes the other may already know there's no hope and deliberately try to make the environment feel worse so the partner would feel so uncomfortable they would be the one to leave. I have seen and experienced this and realised afterwards that it was a well-thought-out plan.

Heads-up, guys! When women are done with giving all the chances under the sun, they are done for good. If they have exhausted every angle to try to improve matters or the issue is too complex to carry on, there are no comebacks.

Women, when men know the woman they are dating is the one, they just know. They know if they want you in their lives for the long term, endless love or just for a short hop. Equally, women make the choice to let the man be the one they want around them.

Some men may be honest enough to tell you they are not ready for anything heavy or that marriage is not their thing. In doing so, they let you know where you stand, and you can make a choice because you know what you have signed up for. You always have the freedom of choice.

I would say, at this point, that whatever decision you come to, make sure you are doing it because it makes you happy. If not, you will find out that the relationship expiration will experience turbulence and an expiry date. Relationships are for a reason, a season or a lifetime. If you know that the relationship is for a season, protect yourself against any hurt you may feel when the purpose has been served.

Hopefully, from the lessons you have learnt, you will move on and forward to a better situation, whether as a single person or a brand-new couple.

They say that 'one man's trash is another man's treasure', but I think this also applies to women.

*'Everything for a time and a season,
a reason, or a lifetime.'*

—*Unknown*

Setting Intentions

As women, we know how we feel when we meet a man. Some of us have all kinds of ideas running around in our heads, wondering if he is the one, what his plans are for the future, or if he likes the same things as us. We wonder if we should call them back and so many other thoughts that we often keep to ourselves for fear of acting too quickly or being too intrusive.

Women may see a man's potential—or lack thereof—in due course, and we make the decision to give it a try or not, as the case may be.

If and when you embark on a new relationship, do so with good or honourable intentions. Remember that the person is someone's daughter or son. Think of how it would be if it you were your own child. Imagine if they were put in a situation by someone who had false intentions. It's surely a position you wouldn't want them to be in. You will have a lot less heartache to deal with if you treated every encounter and every person with decency, honour and respect.

Set your intentions and remember, you can't dictate what their intentions are for you.

Tell your partner what you want, ask if they are open to what you have suggested or stated. You may find that one or both of you change along the way, but whatever happens, make sure it's dealt with from a place of mutual respect.

Life's journey can be one of transformation and improvement.

If you know the other person deserves better than having you in their life, do better. If you don't know how to do better but want to do better, then research how to do it. If you don't want to do better, then move out of that person's way in a considerate, respectful manner, and let them go to someone who will appreciate them.

They say that what is yours will not pass you by.

> *'She was a rose in the hands of those who had no intention of keeping her.'*
>
> —*Rupi Kaur*

Reminders to Self

Be honest with yourself.

What are your intentions for the significant other in your life?

If you know that it's no more than a few dates or a few months, and you know it is not long term, do the other person a favour.

Imagine that your intention and behaviour is the cause of his/her heartache. They will have plenty to tell their friends about you.

It's kinder to let them go to the people with whom they truly belong, especially when you know they deserve better.

Reflections

Take a moment to let these words marinate with you.

What do you feel? Are you joyful, excited, or thoughtful?

What can you do to improve the situation you are in, or if you're not in a situation, what can you do not to let it happen in the first place (forward-thinking)?

Question Time: What do you think?

Write your thoughts here.

Faye Thompson

Words of Affirmation

Look in the mirror and repeat with conviction:

I am at peace.

I am kind.

I am ready for a relationship.

I have good and honest intentions
with my words and my deeds.

I am honourable with my actions
and communication.

I create the intention of a deeply inspired and
respectful relationship.

My intentions will always be pure.

Chapter 5

Build and Support

Take an Interest

In order to build together—a home, a family, or a business—there needs to be a willingness to grow and support each other and to have trust is a must!

For example, if your partner has their own business, you both need that business to do well because it will bring in the finances you both need; how might you help your partner grow it? What will you do to show your support? Will you offer ideas? Can you help advertise the business on social media, through word of mouth, speak proudly of the reliability of the business, create an invoice, type a letter? Do you think it is in both of your best interests, especially if it benefits your future selves together? Remember, it doesn't just have to be a business; it could your partner's career or vocation that you are supporting. How are you helping them progress in that career or vocation? If you truly want a firm foundation in your relationship, it's important to know that your partner's success will ultimately be your success, too. Sometimes this might mean sacrifice or compromise, so discussions about how this support looks and feels to both of you is paramount.

When you are living in the same household, if you both go to work or are self-employed, how do you split the bills in a way that both of you can still survive without taking on too much of a burden or strain on one person if your earnings are not equal? Do you have a pot of money for yourselves as individuals and a bills pot? Do you both have the responsibility to take care of the economic affairs? Do you both save at least ten percent of your earnings first? Have you educated yourselves financially, perhaps looking into exchanging your money into gold or stocks and shares? The choices are yours.

Many moons ago, it was the man's responsibility to be the breadwinner, but nowadays, both people need to share this responsibility, unless you are particularly rich, one wage is sufficient, and your partner or spouse has no issues sharing their wealth.

Be the partner or spouse who shows a genuine interest in your partner's business.

Even a little bit of help doing a small thing can ease the pressure. Two heads are better than one as long as you both have the same vision and shared mission ahead.

This will give you both the opportunity to bounce positive ideas off of one another, and you may come up with something extraordinary! Be encouraging, productive, and industrious together.

Reminders to Self

Teamwork makes the dream work.

**When you plant a seed,
it doesn't bear the fruit overnight.
Give the business time to produce results.**

**Motivate each other to read
about a growth mindset.**

*'If you don't build your dream, someone
will hire you to help them build theirs.'*

—*African proverb*

Reflections

Question Time: How will you show support?

Name five ways you can positively support your partner's business, vocation or career so you will both find it beneficial in whichever way you need it.

1. _____

2. _____

3. _____

4. _____

5. _____

Words of Affirmation

Look in the mirror and repeat with conviction:

I trust you.

I aspire to build a solid foundation together.

I motivate and inspire.

I live in the present, learn from the past, and get ready for the future.

I contribute my talents and knowledge.

I commit to learning new things that will contribute to our progress.

I believe in you.

I got you.

Chapter 6

Commitment

'A successful marriage requires falling in love many times with the same person.'

—Mignon McLaughlin

What is commitment in a relationship?

It is a promise, pledge, vow, obligation, oath, guarantee, and agreement. It is an offer of security, safety, trust, loyalty, and assurance. It is assuming a level of responsibility for your significant other, being answerable and accountable between the two of you.

In my years of growing up, I've heard mixed messages and old wives tales about marriage: 'Three times a bridesmaid, never a bride,' 'When it's supposed to happen it will happen,' 'It's just a piece of paper,' 'It's a fairy-tale romance,' 'It's a match made in heaven,' 'It's commitment till death do us part and happily ever after,' and 'There's no way I'm ever going to get married.' All of them are different points of view about the same thing. Perspectives will differ due to experiences witnessed, perhaps with one's nearest and dearest: is it a match made in heaven or were they marching into war?

As much as I'd love to, I could never sit here and say that marriage is for everyone. I've concluded that some people are meant to be married, and others aren't, and that's okay.

The purpose of commitment in a relationship

Every commitment in a relationship serves its purpose. I've seen people live together for 40-plus years, have children together, and never get married, just as I have seen people get married, and it's over before the year is out.

I have seen childhood sweethearts live amazing married lives, have children, and be there for each other in beautiful, humble, productive ways.

I have seen people in marriages celebrate 30 or 40 years of so-called 'perfect' marriages that go on far longer than they should have, filled with perpetual cheating and disloyalty, eventually ending in bitterness and lies coming to light.

Whilst writing this, as I am not married myself, I thought about the few times when I was asked about engagement or marriage. I was asked at the point of breaking up with the person, but the suggestion had come too late, and I had enough of the distant treatment and lack of love and affection. The person was also extremely critical which made me feel very sad and not good enough.

We have to choose wisely when it comes to taking those vows and hopefully ensure that we have thought carefully about who we choose to be with long term. If there are issues before the "big question" the issues would be there after as well unless they have been fully addressed and a compromise has been reached.

On another occasion, I was asked by an ex-boyfriend with whom I'd been in a three-year relationship over 30 years ago to consider starting over. He wanted to start with courtship and go back to the beginning. He said I was the only person he had considered for marriage, despite having had many girlfriends over that period of time. 30 years had passed in this situation and although he showed his best side, I knew beyond a shadow of a doubt, I was not the same person he had met all those years ago. I didn't forget what happened in that relationship and the reasons it broke down.

I'd grown as a woman, also had children now, and had been through other issues that had given me some personal wisdom.

Well, sometimes I give people the benefit of the doubt; I decided to meet him for lunch. I could see that he had changed a little physically, but what about mentally? All would be revealed after a few probing questions, when I realised that he still had the same underlying issues.

I asked him some questions. For example, I asked him how he felt about the fact that I have male friends. He expressed that he wasn't too sure about that. I knew that I'd come a long way and I wasn't prepared to give up my male friendships. That was the end of that lunch date!

When that relationship ended, it was a huge deal for me. I was young, in my late teens to early twenties, and I knew that it wouldn't work for me. I think he realised that he was unhappy about my decision, but it was his actions that had given him the lesson.

I won't go into the finer details, but all I knew was that I had grown up, and this was not someone to whom I could ever go back. I realised one thing about myself: I don't go back to relationships once I've exhausted all avenues in the relationship.

This has happened to me a few times before with a variety of patterns, so when I'm done, I am done. There's no chasing, no calls, no texts, no nothing. I will not bother you again. The signs say it's a no from me. I will be your friend if I can bear the sight of you, but when it's over, I'm truly over you, and I'll never place my heart in your hands again.

When I think about this situation, it makes me long for a musical interlude.

Music says what the heart feels

Reflections

Question Time: Commitment thought list

What thoughts do you have when it comes to commitments?

Create a commitment thought list below.

What do you do that shows or proves your commitment to your partner?

1. _____

_____

_____

_____

_____

_____

2. _____

_____

_____

_____

_____

_____

3. _____

_____

_____

_____

_____

_____

4. _____
_____
_____
_____
_____

5. _____
_____
_____
_____
_____

6. _____
_____
_____
_____
_____

7. _____
_____
_____
_____

Words of Affirmation

Look in the mirror and repeat with conviction:

I welcome love and commitment
with open arms.

I attract only healthy and loving people
into my life.

I am in a loving, long-lasting,
committed relationship.

I am so grateful for my remarkable relationship.

My love life is a commitment and a priority.

My relationship is worth the commitment.

My love accepts me
and loves me just as I.

Chapter 7

Love and Intimacy

'It's easy to take off all your clothes and have sex. People do it all the time. But opening your soul to someone, letting them into your spirit, thoughts, fears, future, hopes, dreams. That's being naked.'

—Rob Bell

Neglect is poison, attention the fertiliser

If you were friends with the man you love before you became lovers, then you can most likely relate to this quote. Many times, a great love is forged from the bonds of friendship. Make sure that no matter how long you've been together that you also remain friends.

I have one thing to say about this: pay attention to that love that pays attention to you; never take it for granted.

I'm not one for writing poems, however, having attended quite a few poetry nights in Streatham, I felt inspired to write one about love.

Love Is All You Need

Love is all I need when your heart of gold beats next to mine. You are valued by me for your loving kindness.

Your heart beats rhythmically, the sound of the big bang you created within my galactic soul.

The gold dust sparkles from your solar plexus into my heart chakra, bringing out the inner you from your melanin-shaded being.

Our bodies become one and explode from the friction as our temperature rises.

Our souls are synchronised as one with the energy in motion, emotion, devotion, connection.

Bonded together by gravitational attraction.

Breathe—Inhale loving-kindness; exhale warm appreciation.

The sunshine tinted glow of our love meeting in mind, body and soul.

The colour of enlightenment to the higher mind unfolds.

The vibration of creating a love never ending, transforming but never ending.

The visionaries of love illuminated and inspired by the compassion, courage, wisdom, and knowledge within us.

The melanin magic of your body radiates and encapsulates the brilliant shining gem within your solar plexus resonates, and by warming our minds, bodies, and souls, we are empowered, and our confidence grows to love and appreciate each other.

Love is all we need.

Intimacy is the love we create

Intimacy isn't just about the lovemaking; it's about the love we create by showing our vulnerability to one another and being open, honest, and real, without judgement, just listening. When you have warmth in a relationship and good intentions, sexual intimacy can be a very beautiful gift. A genuine gift of love.

Emotional intimacy and familiarity blended with consensual, loving, sexual intimacy can create a passionate and enthused partnership or marriage.

A man and woman's attachment to each other is based on happiness and intimacy. There is an exchange of energy between couples that intertwine on a soul level in our individual energy fields, but we must be careful because auras can weave together. This means that if the person with whom you are sleeping has a negative aura, it interacts with your energy field even if they show something else outwardly. Partners from the past can leave a residue on your aura, so cleansing and cutting ties with the past is necessary. Sometimes our auras can become fragmented, blocked or broken as it's possible for others to steal our energy but also for us to take on others' negative energy too. It's possible to heal broken auras, and this is something I suggest is something to research or take into consideration when choosing a partner or even interacting with someone. Does their energy make you feel expansive and positive, or does it disturb and disrupt your own energy field and sense of peace? As a suggestion, take a look at chakra healing, specifically the sacral chakra, using energy-clearing meditation such as binaural beats and specific crystals.

You can also use music as a way for your soul to express itself. It's a great way to heal and express our emotions. I love music and spoken word as they express in melody things my heart would love to say (without feeling 100% embarrassed telling someone face-to-face). How does music make you feel?

'Is it the way you love me, baby?'

—*Jill Scott*

Reflections

Look into your partner's eyes. Take a nice long look.

Stay in that precious moment. Feel the sensation of love rising in you. Are you brave enough to savour that moment?

When your two souls' energy become intertwined like DNA strands, say out loud or think in your head: 'I feel your energy, you feel mine. We become one flesh. Emotion. Energy in motion.'

It's okay to be silent with your partner, hold hands, and interlock fingers.

Let your hands send positive, loving vibrations to each other.

If you already have great intimacy, that's awesome. It signifies a treasured commitment.

Loving intimacy, that familiarity, closeness, and understanding, consists of both knowing and expressing what you enjoy without inhibition.

Value your time and consistency together.

Question Time: Intimacy and honesty

What's really stopping you from intimacy and connection? Be straightforward and honest.

Do you want intimacy to return, or are you quite happy keeping it guarded? If you are happy not being intimate, what impact do you think that will have on your significant other?

What ideas do you have to create more time for intimacy, or how could you make an intimate environment for you and your significant other?

1. _____
   _____
   _____
   _____
   _____
   _____

2. _____
   _____
   _____
   _____
   _____
   _____

3. _____
   _____
   _____
   _____
   _____

I Got You

4. _____
_____
_____
_____
_____
_____

5. _____
_____
_____
_____
_____
_____

Words of Affirmation

Look in the mirror and repeat with conviction:

I am committed.

I am consistent.

I am devoted.

I am faithful.

I am loyal.

I am relaxed.

I am trustworthy.

Chapter 8

Respect

'If you want to be respected, you must respect yourself.'

—*Spanish proverb*

Respect fosters appreciation and admiration

When there is respect in a relationship, there is a feeling of deep appreciation and admiration for another person, prompted by their abilities, qualities, and achievements. When you show you can respect another person's feelings, wishes, or rights, it encourages them to build trust and respect for you.

Treating each other with mutual respect shows that you value that person as an individual and not just as something attached to you. Respect is not rocket science. If there was only one rule, it should be that we all respect each other. I feel this would make the world would be a better place.

Getting your point across to your partner should not require shouting, neither should it mean that you shouldn't say anything at all. Walking on eggshells indicates that respect isn't present in the relationship as you are constantly in fear of how the other person may react to you expressing your thoughts and feelings. This isn't healthy. You need to find a healthy way to communicate your needs, wants, thoughts, and feelings in a space where there is respect and safety.

With respect in mind, treat each other as you would want your children to be treated when they embark on a relationship. Kindness, compassion and deep listening can be transformative for your relationship.

Reminders to Self

Respect each other's privacy.

Respect each other's feelings.

Respect each other's families.

Respect timekeeping.

Keeping your word/promises shows respect.

Respect positive thoughts and beliefs.

Respect one another's differences.

Respect conversations and confidentiality.

Be consistently consistent.

Reflections

Question Time: Showing respect

What do you do to show respect in a relationship?

_____
_____
_____
_____
_____

Does your spouse/partner/significant other have the same or similar views as you?

_____
_____
_____
_____
_____

Does this have an impact on your relationship, and how?

What are your thoughts?

Write down some of the things you respect or make up some of your own 'respect' affirmations.some of your own 'respect' affirmations.

1. _____

2. _____

3. _____

4. _____

5. _____

_____

_____

_____

_____

6. _____

_____

_____

_____

_____

7. _____

_____

_____

_____

_____

_____

'R.E.S.P.E.C.T.
Find out what it means to me.'

—*Aretha Franklin*

Words of Affirmation

Look in the mirror and repeat with conviction:

I respect myself.

I respect you.

I respect choices that are made with the best intentions.

I respect understanding.

I respect honesty.

I respect differences.

I respect freedom.

'Without respect, there is no love.'

—*Unknown*

Chapter 9

Forgiveness

'It's not an easy journey to get to a place where you forgive people, but it's such a powerful place because it frees you.'

—Tyler Perry

Holding onto resentment is a toxic practice

At some point in your life, you may come across a person or people who hurt your feelings. This can be the most painful thing you endure. Thoughts of the incident can engulf your mind whilst the person who hurt you walks away and gets on with their life. Sometimes they don't even know they have hurt you, but sometimes, they do.

The energy this creates within your personal being causes bitterness, regret, and draining thoughts. For some, the constant replay can lead to depression. When this happens, the person takes possession of your personal mental space with their hurtful ways.

How dare they!

A lack of forgiveness is, however, toxic to your wellbeing. The person you can't or won't forgive successfully disempowers you. You may not realise that holding onto the resentment does not serve your mental wellbeing, and it has no effect on the offender.

You should do your best not to blame yourself because sometimes, it is not you. There are three sides to a story: yours, theirs, and the truth. Letting feelings go when they make you feel bad will help you move forward and leave things in the past where they belong.

Be mindful. Stay in the present. Try not to dwell on harmful thoughts. Don't keep walking with that suitcase packed full of burdens.

To forgive is to replace negative emotions or feelings and bring them to a place of peace. If you hold on to the negative energy and/or memories, it will hold you back from progressing and moving forward.

Love, prayer, and forgiveness are always available when you tap into them. Today, wake up with the intention of being good to yourself. Fill your own cup. Let it overflow with the amazing thoughts and joy you deserve.

> *'Darkness cannot drive out darkness; only light can do that. Hate cannot drive out hate; only love can do that.'*
>
> —*Dr Martin Luther King*

Forgiveness is intentional

Forgiving doesn't mean forgetting or condoning the misdemeanour. Forgiving someone is intentional. It does not focus on the outcome. Once implemented, let it go because the time you're wasting is your own; the other person is happily getting on with their life.

Forgiveness expresses a change of feelings. It is you choosing to empower yourself and release negative and destructive emotions holding you in your pain.

'Forgiveness is not always easy. At times, it feels more painful than the wound we suffered to forgive the one that inflicted it. And yet, there is no peace without forgiveness.'

—*Marianne Williamson*

Create a ground-breaking, healthier, more successful story

Make up your mind to set positive intentions and to attract and have a more positive circle of people in your life. I did this about four years ago. I set intentions and clear requirements, started a new journey, and have met some wonderful people along the way.

In the past, you may have had pieces of your heart broken or insulted, but those days are gone. There's someone out there, bringing peace with them. I strongly believe there's someone for everyone, and that person will come when you least expect it.

That person may not even be in the same country as you, but they are out there, hopefully setting intentions for the same thing.

So, don't give up because of someone else's poor behaviour. Continue to do you. Make yourself into the best version of yourself. There could be someone praying to meet you, as well, and you will be perfect for that person just the way you are.

My mum always says, 'You never know who's around the corner.' With that said, it's time to embark upon a brand-new chapter, a renewal or rebirth, whatever you wish to call it, and there's no time like the present. It's time to write your next chapter or volume are you ready?

> *'My sunshine has come No more rain in this cloud.'*
>
> —*Angie Stone*

Reflections

If you feel that you are unable to forgive or feel that forgiveness is only from a higher source, can you accept what has happened and move forward so you will not be chained to a time or event that no longer serves you?

Question Time: Showing forgiveness

How do you define forgiveness?

_____
_____
_____
_____
_____
_____
_____
_____

Why is forgiveness important to you?

How do you think forgiveness will better your life?

Faye Thompson

Words of Affirmation

Look in the mirror and repeat with conviction:

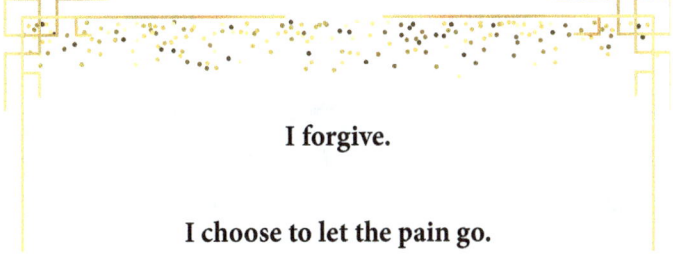

I forgive.

I choose to let the pain go.

I embrace a new and more purposeful chapter.

I accept the lesson and make a change.

I deserve better.

I deserve peace of mind.

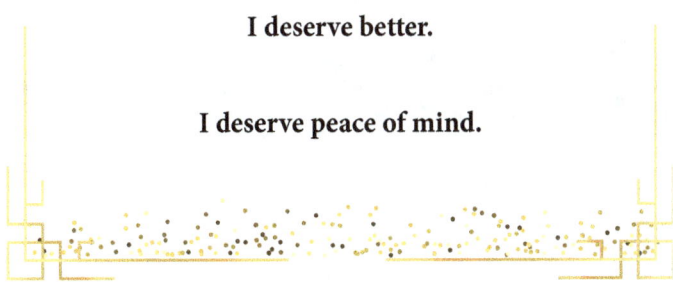

Chapter 10

Gratitude

Appreciate your partner

When your partner is a consistent blessing in your life, show your gratitude. Appreciate them in whatever way you can. Tell them, show them, but somehow, let them know as it can make all the difference.

Let's ask ourselves a question right now: how often do we notice the little things our partners do for us, and do you remember to thank them? What is a little thing?

It could simply be picking up your favourite treat on the way home, a caring note on the fridge door, cooking your favourite meal and dessert, tickets for a show, game, or movie, or doing the dishes. Everyone will have their own little thing that makes them feel like someone thought of them and that they still feel valued in your life.

Some people can wholeheartedly say that they acknowledge and appreciate the things people do for them, while others will need to think about it.

Children live what they learn

In my daily life, I guide and observe little children, and let's face it, most of the habits and personalities and triggers we have are based on our seven-year-old selves. Children learn what they live and live what they learn.

Guide and teach your children manners and in positive ways that will carry them through their lives. Building resilience is also key. I say this because appreciation and gratitude is something homegrown, and it sometimes takes a big change to undo or create another kind of you. This reminds me of the story, 'A Christmas Carol', in which seeing the past, present, and future made Scrooge change his ways.

Appreciation is something to practice every single day and being grateful will serve you well.

To get started, you could try keeping a journal and embark upon a gratitude challenge for at least 21 days.

I can't stress it enough when I say that appreciation is a must and saying 'thank you' is only two small words. Saying, 'I appreciate all you do,' can carry a lot of power. It can make someone feel so loved.

Growing up, I was told that manners would carry you far in this world. Guess what? It costs zero pounds—yes, it's totally free! Who loves free stuff? Can I get a 'yes'?

No one should ever feel they are entitled not to be thankful or show their appreciation because they have been in a relationship for months or years, which doesn't mean you never need to say please or thanks ever again. It's just rude not to, don't you think?

Be a role model. Show how it's done. Emphasise the good things in your relationship, and you will attract more of the same. Focusing on gratitude will attract more gratitude, and if it doesn't, you may need to think about whether the person really respects you.

The more you notice frustrating and irritating habits, the more they will manifest.

Reminders to Self

Show gratitude to your partner.

Teach children manners so they
carry them throughout their lives.

Showing manners shows appreciation.

Be a positive role model
by focusing on gratitude.

Focusing on gratitude
attracts more gratitude.

Reflections

Question Time: Showing appreciation and gratitude

What do you appreciate about your partner?

1. _____

2. _____

3. _____

List things for which you are grateful in life:

1. _____

_____

_____

_____

_____

_____

2. _____

_____

_____

_____

_____

_____

3. _____

_____

_____

_____

_____

_____

How might you show yourself appreciation and/or gratitude?

1. _____

2. _____

3. _____

How might you show your partner appreciation and/or gratitude?

1. _____

2. _____

3. _____

Words of Affirmation

Look in the mirror and repeat with conviction:

**I am grateful.
I appreciate who you are
and what you mean to me.**

**I am grateful for your
thoughts and inspirations
that help me move forward
positively and powerfully.**

**I am grateful that you have shown me
a way to discover my higher potential.**

Words of Affirmation

Look in the mirror and repeat with conviction:

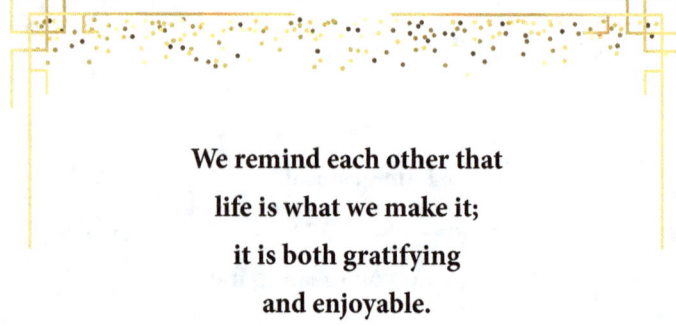

**We remind each other that
life is what we make it;
it is both gratifying
and enjoyable.**

**I am thankful you find
the strength to support me
when I'm not the
best version of myself.**

I am appreciative.

Chapter 11

Reliability

'Call when you say you will, show up when you say you will, and deliver what you say you will. Inconsistency destroys trust and trust is the foundation of all relationships.'

—Paul Carrick Brunson

The significance of dependability in a relationship

I am a person who requires reliability. There's something in me that makes me not want to let people down, simply because I know the feeling of being let down, and it's very disappointing.

Understandably, circumstances can crop up; however, when you notice a pattern of behaviour, the mind can take you to another place: is this person just making excuses, and what is the problem? If there is an underlying problem, let's discuss it.

As a part of my personality—although I am learning to say 'no' when I'm pressed for time in certain situations—the only time I will not show up for something I've already planned is if there's a good reason, such as an illness or travelling for a distance and my car has broken down the moment I get in it (this is a true story!).

Dependability in a relationship makes for a strong foundation on which to build. It means that your partner can count on you and feel a sense of security. I'm not implying that you take them for granted or pretend like you can't do things for yourself, but they should know that there is someone else in their life and that you are the person they can contact, and you consistently support and care for them and vice versa.

> *'The ability to show reliability
> grows another wonderful fruit
> called 'trustworthiness".*
>
> —Unknown

When people let you down at the last minute, it can make people go into 'panic mode', and for whatever reason, can become overwhelming if there's no immediate solution. They may have to get creative and think of a plan B or even C!

Knowing that someone is reliable is a big asset in all walks of life, as that person will show you commitment, trustworthiness, and loyalty.

Reminders to Self

Dependability is an important
foundation of a good relationship.

Being dependable
builds security in a relationship.

Being reliable shows commitment,
trustworthiness, and loyalty
in a relationship.

Reflections

Honestly, if you say you're going to do something, make sure you do it. Your word is your bond.

It's not nice to let people down. They will remember it and talk about it, sometimes repetitively.

It can mean all the difference as to whether anyone will ever trust you again.

Question Time: Reliability and dependability

What does reliability mean to you? Make seven points.

1. _____

_____

_____

2. _____

_____

_____

3. _____
_____
_____
_____

4. _____
_____
_____
_____

5. _____
_____
_____
_____

6. _____
_____
_____
_____

7. _____
_____
_____
_____

How do you show your reliability?

When someone is unreliable, how does it make you feel?

What can you do to improve your reliability?

Words of Affirmation

Look in the mirror and repeat with conviction:

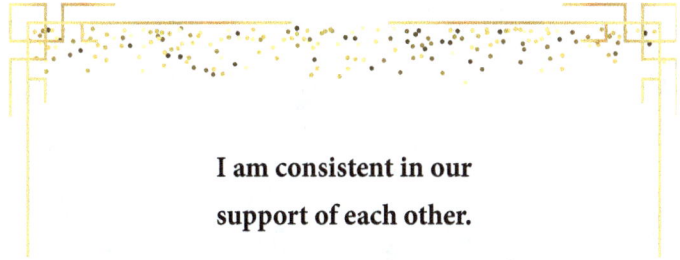

I am consistent in our support of each other.

I am reliable.

I am a good, honest person.

I am respectful and reliable about the things that matter to you.

I am considerate.

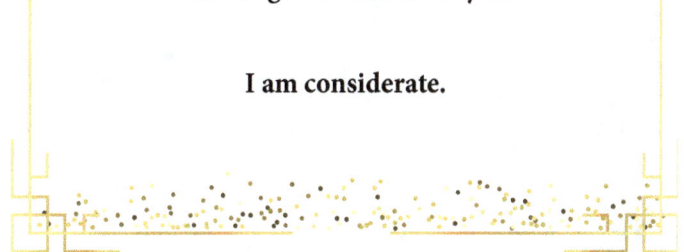

Chapter 12

Love

*'Being deeply loved by someone gives you strength
while loving someone deeply gives you courage.'*

—*Lao Tzu*

What is love?

There are four kinds of love according to the dictionary.

Storge:

Empathy bond – this is liking someone because there is the presence of familiarity and fondness it is described as the most natural love for example the love of a parent and child or other family members. There is no coercion, and it is emotive because of the familiarity of fondness.

Agape:

Unconditional love. This is God understanding that no matter what happens the love will always be there regardless of the transformations or transitions that take place. It is regarded as a selfless love.

Eros:

Eros is sexual desire, loving the physical. Eros is the passion, lust, and/or romance. Eros, the love felt between lovers and is the sensual love between people who are attracted to each sexually.

Philla:

Affectionate Love without romantic attraction. It is the love shared between friends and family members. When people share the same respect and values as each other. This type of love is kind, encouraging and affectionate. It makes a genuine friendship.

Manifesting love

Tapping away on this laptop keyboard, I'm thinking: what on earth do I know about love? I ask myself with the eyeball emoji staring back at me, rolling its eyes. Love is a personal experience and journey, and it manifests in different ways.

Love is always the answer, and we would do well to remember that everyone has a different way of expressing it. At times, we miss how it's shown by someone else and how it's received, then we get cross with the other person for not showing it in a way we recognise based on our expectations.

What I mean by this is that some people want to see love, others want to feel it, and some may want to hear it.

It's been left up to the individual to work out how their significant other expresses this four-letter word that so many shy away from. Love shows our vulnerability. Some of us have shown it repeatedly, and some of us will take the love we had/have for someone to our graves. I know several women and men who have had broken hearts, and they are not prepared to let their guards down ever again.

It's not the love that hurts; it the disrespect, the lack of trust, the disloyalty, the arguments, the silent treatment, the neglect, the lack of attention, and the being taken for granted.

The healing power of love

Love does not hurt; love heals. The negative energy that can arise from the opposite of love is what hurts. No one enjoys being hurt. Sadly, some people have been hurt so much they cannot let go of the hurt and start a fresh page with a new chapter and a new connection in case it happens again. They push away and sabotage potential partners because of the chains and cages around their hearts, and they refuse to let other people in, just in case.

This disappointment needs addressing and healing. Some people may choose therapy to help remove the self-sabotage and blockages in their subconscious minds.

Therapies like reiki, neuro-linguistic programming, energy alignment methods, mindfulness, and filling one's own cup aid in the lessening or removal of these blockages.

Others go down the 'drowning it out' path—sex, drinking, drug use, gambling, or holidaying it away—avoiding the real issue or avoiding social gatherings. Whatever the pathway, when you wake up, the problem will still be there. It may numb the pain for a minute; however, the root cause is still there, and more than likely, needs immediate attention, like a bad tooth in need of a root canal.

This may cost a person like a root canal, but at some point, they won't be able to hide the feelings, and the patterns won't go unnoticed. Patterns repeat until you find a way to stop and change your mindset. When you have love in your heart and the sense that someone has connected to your soul, your emotional being leaves you open to feel something amazing. However, people are scared because they also equate love with hurt. Love doesn't hurt; poor actions do. Let your love rise from your deepest human principles. Be kind, caring, and nurturing.

When you receive love, treasure it. It might be all that person has to give.

Whether verbal, physical, emotional, or psychological, if it creates feelings the opposite of love, it probably hasn't come from a place of love.

Biblical thoughts about love for those who enjoy reading from scripture:

'Love is patient, love is kind.

It does not envy, it does not boast, it is not proud…

It is not self-seeking, it is not easily angered,
it keeps no record of wrongs.

Love does not delight in evil but rejoices with the truth

It always protects, always trusts, always hopes,
always perseveres.

Love never fails.'

(1 Corinthians 13; 4, 7-8)

*'If you find someone you love in this life,
hang on to that love.'*

—Princess Diana

Reminders to Self

Everyone expresses love differently.

Showing love shows vulnerability.

Love doesn't hurt;
disrespect, a lack of trust,
disloyalty, arguments,
silent treatments,
neglect, a lack of attention,
and being taken for granted
in a relationship do.

Be kind, caring, and nurturing.

When you receive love, treasure it.

Reflections

Question Time: Showing your love

In what ways do you show your significant other that you love them?

1. _____

2. _____

3. _____

In what ways does your significant other make you feel loved?

1. _____
   _____
   _____
   _____

2. _____
   _____
   _____
   _____

3. _____
   _____
   _____
   _____

Words of Affirmation

Look in the mirror and repeat with conviction:

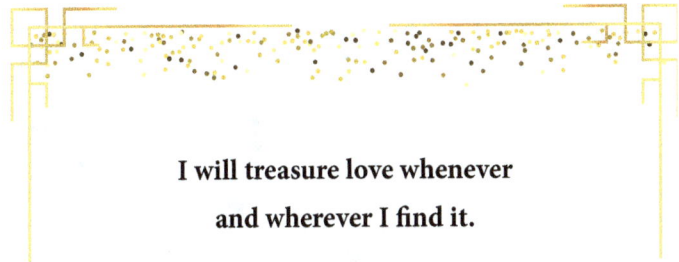

**I will treasure love whenever
and wherever I find it.**

I will be kind.

I will be caring.

I will be nurturing.

Chapter 13

Honesty

'Life is about balance. Be kind, but don't let people abuse you. Trust, but don't be deceived. Be content, but never stop improving yourself'.

—Zig Ziglar

Never mistreat anyone.

Be prepared for real honesty; if you can't be honest in your relationship, what's the point of being in it? Openly and honestly express your feelings to your significant other. Be mindful that you use kind words. When there are barricades on your heart, it confines you from receiving the enjoyment of loving fully from another person.

Honesty can make you feel fragile or show your weaknesses; however, even if the conversation makes you feel uncomfortable or anxious, when both of you can come from a mindset of mutual respect, active listening, and not blow up at each other, fight the urge to become defensive—it can deepen your connection and show the appreciation you have for each other.

If there is a wall in a relationship, there needs to be a way of breaking it down so you can rebuild with an improved approach.

If you want to progress, be able to sit down with each other in a mindset of authentic trust, and both of you can speak your truth. Real sincere honesty is one of the many things that make a successful relationship.

Speak your truth sensitively without blame. Sometimes it's an uncomfortable conversation.

You could try using 'I feel' sentences (e.g., I feel upset that we didn't get to meet as planned). See how or if your significant other's response changes.

Make sure you have the facts and evidence before assuming there's a problem.

Although intuition—which is the ability to understand something instinctively without the need for conscious effort—is real, for the most part, sometimes, we are just waiting for an honest conversation so we can either find a solution and move forward.

Reminders to Self

Embrace honesty in your relationships.

Use kind words when expressing
your feelings to your significant other.

Speak your truth
without assigning blame;
be sensitive in uncomfortable
conversations.

Be sure to have all the facts
before making assumptions about
your partner's behaviour.

Reflections

Question Time: Personal check in

What are your thoughts at this moment?

What triggers you to make assumptions?

___

Have your assumptions ever been correct?

___

Do you trust your gut instincts? Why or why not?

___

What can you do to ensure you don't make assumptions?

___

Words of Affirmation

Look in the mirror and repeat with conviction:

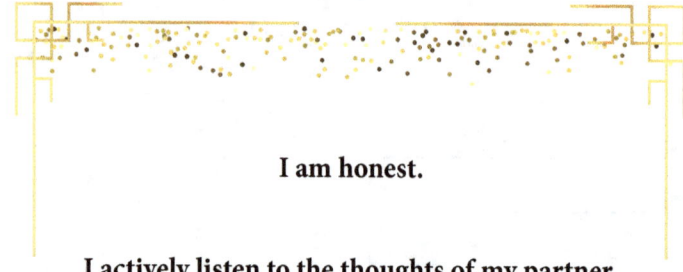

I am honest.

I actively listen to the thoughts of my partner.

I speak from a place of love.

I find out the facts first.

**I am honest with myself and others
and keep my promises
to myself and others.**

Chapter 14

Communication

'I think our biggest problem is a lack of real, honest communication between Black men and Black women. A lot of men talk amongst men, and a lot of women speak amongst women.'

—Hill Harper

Communication is a two-way street

Find the time or make an effort to actively listen to what each other says without interrupting. This should go without saying really: show respect and be respectful when engaging in your conversations. We all get frustrated and angry, but see if you can effectively master and think about the words you use with each other.

When you're in a state of anger, you often say things you don't mean or approach a situation in an off-putting way, meaning that the person may clam up and not have the discussion with you at all. The opposite, when everything is blown out of proportion, may also occur.

Neither way can bring a positive outcome, as important conversations will be left unsaid, or they will say every mean thought, leaving someone to apologise.

Think about what you say. Does communication with your partner inspire, boost, encourage, or motivate them or does it provoke,discourage, criticise, and dishearten? Speak from a loving place as often as possible.

Don't shy away from compliments

Some people are not always used to receiving compliments or positive comments and may even say something negative to shy away from it. Even if it's hard. Try to accept what is being said and remember that they took the time to notice something positive and had the courage and openness to share it with you. Be open to give and receive compliments.

Perhaps it's you that's able to express yourself using encouraging, loving words, and your partner feels as if it is too much. They may not be used to that level of expression because it's new to them.

When you can express yourself lovingly and listen for the response or lack of from the other person, you can begin to see their thought process.

I have opened my heart and laid it on the table only to realise that someone did not feel the same way, and that was it—no more calls, seeing neither hide nor hair of them! I can look at it as a blessing now, but back then, it seemed like doom and gloom. The reality was that we were not on the same page, and I guess that we had no intention of ever being on it. It didn't make my life any worse; in fact, it was a blessing in disguise.

A word from the wise is that the opposite can and does happen, where you lay that same heart out, and the person stays around for more than a season and hopefully a lifetime. It is said that anything that is yours will not pass you by.

Resolve your conflicts

If your relationship still means something to you, find a way through persistence, perseverance, and patience to sustain communication.

Sometimes, our learnt behaviours from childhood get in the way of our communication skills, and we subconsciously remember the negative responses from our early upbringing that has remained in our subconscious minds. Hopefully, you will eventually realise that this doesn't serve a purpose in your adult life.

Certain statements may do more harm than people realise. For example, to say, 'Little children should be seen and not heard,' 'Only speak when you're spoken to,' don't bode well for the subconscious mind. Someone who is anxious, quiet, or reserved may not get to voice their feelings or opinions and therefore never be able to have those all-important conversations to move a relationship forward. Their voice goes unheard and resentment builds. They do not want to spoil the vibe. They may not like the sound of their voice or be too scared to say the 'wrong thing' for fear of repercussions or judgment from others.

There are others in this world who have no filters whatsoever, and everything on their minds is spoken. This can also be too much, said without understanding, or said in anger or bitterness.

The DONT'S

- X Don't stonewall (silent treatment) your partner—this is not an alternative to fixing or trying to resolve an issue.

- X Don't decide on extended silence—a few hours, maybe, but weeks and weeks? That's something else. This can backfire on you as being silent for a lengthier time than usual is not productive.

- X Consider that the other person may have not genuinely known what the problem was between you because it had never been discussed.

- X Toy with the idea that the other person is not a mind reader, and their values or upbringing may not be the same as yours.

- X Don't be manipulating, controlling, or use powers of persuasion and anger to get your way.

- X Don't try to change someone—everyone is born to be themselves.

How deep is it?

If the person with whom you are romantically involved, in your heart of hearts, is not to your liking, then you have a few choices.

Tolerate that on which you are not keen. Ask yourself: is it that deep? Is it going to ruin your world? Are pants and towels on the floor deep? Is the toothpaste lid left off kind of deep? Is this a more serious habit?

Do you leave, walk out the door, burn the bridge, and don't look back if you absolutely cannot tolerate any part of the situation that affects you emotionally, mentally, or physically, especially if it doesn't support your values or morals?

If you are doing well with and for your partner, don't let the spark burn out.

At least once a month, save a little money for your 'entertainment fund', a pleasurable and memorable night in or out.

Think about how you met the person and all the special memories you created together. These memorable occasions shouldn't go out the window, as it's what brought you two together in the first place.

Even if you have children, there's always an opportunity to do something if you make it a priority. Set aside a date or a day every month to touch base and do something together—no phones or technology, just your undivided attention.

*'The biggest communication problem
is that we do not listen to understand.
We listen to reply.'*

—*Stephan R Covey*

Faye Thompson

Reminders to Self

Do not speak to your partner in anger;
be mindful to communicate
from a place of love.

Be opened to giving
and receiving comments.

Communicate to resolve conflicts.

Choose your battles.

Reflections

Question Time: Communication in relationships

Can I tolerate this for an extended period in my life?

Suggest how to make things better. Is the issue detrimental to your relationship? How can you lovingly communicate this to your significant other?

How do you rate your speaking and communication skills?

	YES	NO	SOMETIMES
I'm an excellent and effective communicator when I speak with my partner.	☐	☐	☐
I get my point across without getting angry with my partner.	☐	☐	☐
I consider myself quiet and reasonable when speaking with my partner.	☐	☐	☐
I could be more thoughtful when I speak to my partner.	☐	☐	☐
I don't like talking to my partner.	☐	☐	☐

Why did you give yourself this rating?

1. _____
2. _____
3. _____
4. _____
5. _____

What improvements can you make in terms of the speaking aspect of communication?

What's important to you regarding the speaking aspect of communication with your partner/spouse?

When can you free up your schedule for quality-time communication?

Do you actively listen to your partner—this means no distractions (i.e., phone/tv/iPad off or on silent)?

_____
_____
_____
_____

When you listen, are you able to repeat back the key points they made so you are clear about what they are saying?

_____
_____
_____
_____

What mutual date nights/days can you line up (this doesn't have to be outside the home or expensive)?

_____
_____
_____
_____

I Got You

When someone values you, they will take the time to actively listen to your side of the story.

_____

_____

_____

_____

_____

'Can we talk for a minute?'

—Usher

Faye Thompson

Words of Affirmation

Look in the mirror and repeat with conviction:

We/I communicate in the
most respectful way.

We/I enjoy an active life together.

I communicate without bitterness.

I communicate without bringing up the past.

I communicate in a considerate manner.

I communicate from a place of love.

I communicate with kindness
and consideration.

Chapter 15

Trust

'Trust enables you to put your deepest feelings and fears in the palm of your partner's hand, knowing they will be handled with care.'

—*Carl S. Avery*

Trust your intuition

Letting someone know that you trust them sometimes means more to some people than saying that you love them. When trust has walked out the door, don't be surprised when the key is turned in the lock and you can't get back in.

Trust is an important aspect of any relationship or friendship.

Bob Marley sang, 'Only your friend knows your secrets, so only he can reveal it.'

This simply means that if you only confide in one person, and you hear about it outside of the relationship, there's only one person that could have spoken about the situation to someone else.

When you say, 'I trust you' in a relationship, you openly declare your faith in the other person and genuinely feel that they have made good, reliable choices, and you are not worried about confiding in them because he will keep his word.

Building trust in relationships

There are ways to build trust in a relationship. One of the most meaningful ways for me is to say what you mean and mean what you say. I love reliability—it helps me feel valued.

Personally speaking, being flaky doesn't work well for me. If I say I'm going to meet you for lunch at 12 o'clock, I will be there.

People know when they are avoiding situations or being flaky, and the onus is on them to be honest about their feelings. It also shows that you are able to be respectful and express your feelings without fear of judgement for your past. We all have a past, and sometimes we make choices that don't serve us well; however, these are journeys that put us on other paths for the time being. Hopefully, now you will be able to make better and wiser choices.

For some, building trust might mean taking risks together. Perhaps you've decided to start a business, and you feel confident enough to team up with your significant other and run the business together.

You may be in a position of trust in the business, so stick to deadlines or handling the finances of the business. Your role might be to make sure you deal with tasks in a timely manner and don't run off with the money.

You may be in a position of trust in the business, so stick to deadlines or handling the finances of the business; your role will be to make sure you deal with tasks in a timely manner and so don't run off with the money!

Trust your intuition to make the most of your opportunities to communicate.

Reminders to Self

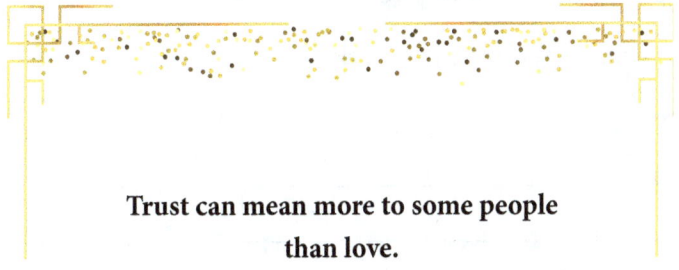

Trust can mean more to some people than love.

Trust is an important aspect of any and all relationships.

Say what you mean and mean what you say.

Reflections

Question Time: Trusting yourself and others

Do you trust yourself in your relationship?

_____
_____
_____
_____
_____

How do you show that you are trustworthy?

_____
_____
_____
_____
_____

Do you trust your partner/husband/wife? If yes, why? If no, why not?

If the trust has gone, what can your significant other do to earn it back? Can they ever earn it back?

How does your partner show that they are trustworthy?

Words of Affirmation

Look in the mirror and repeat with conviction:

I trust my intuition.

I trust my decisions.

I trust my instincts.

I trust that you will communicate with me honestly.

I trust in myself that I will respect our relationship.

**I trust I have our best interests at heart.
I trust you.**

Chapter 16

The Languages of Love

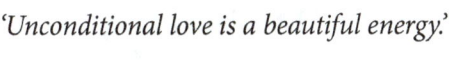

'Unconditional love is a beautiful energy.'

—*Unknown*

Love is valuable in our lives

One of our basic needs is the hierarchy of life. It's a beautiful thing to love and feel it is returned. There's nothing like it. It's one of the greatest things you can experience. When you have someone that reflects love energy back to you every day, you can feel your life thriving or being motivated.

It is possible to love without love being returned; it's always much more restorative when you are. On the positive side, love can make us feel safe and secure, to know and feel, and our hearts are being cared for, not just by us. Love is shown in many ways—how do you show yours, and does it reflect on your partner?

The Five Love Languages

'The Five Love Languages: How to express heartfelt commitment to your mate' were brought to light by author Gary Chapman. He shows us, in an insightful way that we all need love in our own special way. Sometimes we are mismatched and think the other person doesn't really love us because they don't show love in the way we want to receive it and in the way we think we should give and receive love. We need to show love to our significant other the way they like it not the way we like to receive it!

Quality Time

Quality time is the act of spending time with the people you love. Giving your partner undivided attention—no TV, phones, or other electronic devices—is a powerful way to connect with them. There are plenty of ways to spend quality time together, whether inside or outside the home, such as meeting for a drink or dinner and chat, cooking, or working out as a couple or a family, planning away days with no outside disturbances, couple or family holidays, or setting aside time to listen to your partner without distractions such as social media or work. Everyone is on a busy schedule these days, but don't just try to fit someone in. How much do you value their presence in your life?

Make an effort to schedule a dedicated special night in or out, especially if you know they will try to drop everything to spend some time with you. Time is something you just cannot get back. It doesn't cost anything. It can be the most appreciated thing you can give to your significant other. Having one-on-one time creates special shared memories. Take the time to listen or focus on shared goals or to just be in their company on a weekend break, uninterrupted, phones away, no distractions. Have fun!

People make time for what's important to them. Your partner will realise how much of a priority they are in your life just by your actions. Devote time and attention for each other, which will make a huge difference to your communication and relationship.

Acts of Service

Acts of service occur when your partner sees something you need and demonstrates their love by doing something for you that's not necessarily romantic, but it meets a practical need. It's the art of doing something from your heart, making their favourite food or drink, cleaning the car, hoovering, and/or doing the dishes without prompting, buying lunch or dinner and taking it to their place of work. Doing something for your loved one without being asked is a sign of care and attention.

Ways to demonstrate acts of service

Your beloved is sick with flu—what can you do to help them? You're out, so go shopping for them. Bring them back some food. Better still, make them some wholesome homemade soup or a rejuvenating home remedy to perk him up. Find out how your partner likes to be treated when they are ill — having company vs being left in peace.

Whatever you decide, try not to be scornful. You might be sick one day and in need of assistance. Do whatever you choose, but do it with love from the heart, and not just for brownie points.

Physical Touch

Physical touch is the act of touching someone from your heart. It's a love that is non-verbal, including hugging, cuddling, sensual gratification, intimacy, neck rubs, back-scratching, massages, kissing, tickling (sometimes a matter of choice), holding hands, stroking hair, and/or dancing closely together, and it has a lot to do with longing to feel and safe and seen. Some people feel valued and loved when they receive physical touches from their partners. For them, it strengthens their bonds. Some people are born with an enormous need for affection and a definite need to give it. Show authentic care for each other.

Ways to demonstrate physical touch

Physical touch doesn't always have to mean grand gestures or kissing your partner passionately in public. If you are uncomfortable with huge public displays of affection, you can still use physical touch in a subtler way. For example, gently touching the arm, hand, or shoulder can demonstrate concern and care in public, and not just in private.

Your significant other is someone of whom you are proud, and it's not shameful or embarrassing to show it. Hold hands or walk arm in arm.

Humans need oxytocin. Oxytocin is also known as the 'love hormone'. It is released in the brain and in the initial stages of a relationship it tends to rise and when we are being intimate. For a mother and her newborn, it assists with their bonding.

In men, it is used for sperm motility and affects the production of testosterone. Oxytocin is grouped with the happiness hormones; this has a productive effect on moods and emotions.

The loving cuddles and intimacy, we receive activate feelings of trust, bonding, calm, and wellbeing. What happens if there's no one to hug? Well, we can always get it from vitamins and minerals in food.

Vitamin D is the sunshine and happy vitamin; lack of it can cause depression and low moods. Magnesium is a receptor for oxytocin. We can eat dark chocolate, pumpkin, mushrooms, spinach. Vitamin C found in many well-known foods like oranges and peppers etc help produce oxytocin.

Overall, oxytocin helps with social interactions. If you are lacking in oxytocin, you may find that it's challenging to communicate with others, or you generally feel low. Also, stress makes your cortisol hormones rise and your oxytocin level lowers.

Free hugs anyone?

Receiving Gifts

The gesture of a gift is something some people need to feel loved, appreciated, or to know they are being thought about. When you are with a partner whose love language is receiving gifts, it's not necessarily about the most expensive or lavish gifts you can buy, but the thought behind what you buy. Gifts should come from the heart, personalised and meaningful gifts, keepsakes, or memorable items show thoughtfulness and care.

Ways to demonstrate the art of gift buying

Let's say your significant other loves playing snooker, but they are fed up with the dodgy cues they must use when they are out. When/if they happen to mention it to you, make a mental note of it, so the next time you are scrolling through an online store or out and about at the town centre, how about getting them their own, personalised cue? It will be a thoughtful act, and you will have taken your partner's interests into consideration. Perhaps your partner had been having a hard time at work recently—why not go ahead and give them a voucher for a spa day? Perhaps you can even include yourself in the pampering session.

Words of Affirmation

Words of affirmation are positive words used to express love, appreciation, or affection. It's the art of speaking from your heart, using spoken words of appreciation, compliment, love notes, letters, or poetry with positive reflection. For some people, verbal communication is key. Some people need to hear how you feel about them, as it reaffirms the relationship and establishes a deeper connection. Words can be written; others are spoken. Either way, it's about the communication of feelings.

To be acknowledged and given a compliment is embarrassing for some, but don't let compliments make you feel that way. Accept compliments gladly, but in a humble manner. Saying 'thank you' with a smile is often enough.

Ways to demonstrate words of affirmation

- To be told 'I love you,' 'I care about you,' 'I trust you,' can mean the world to someone. If you feel this, tell the person so, and make sure you mean what you say.'

- Write a Post-it Note and leave it on the door before you go out or send a simple text to let the person know you are thinking of him. This can make all the difference demonstrate appreciation and make your partner feel valued.

- Can't find the words? Dedicate a song to the person on the radio or make a playlist of songs that lets him know how you feel about them.

- Actively listen to each other without interrupting. Listen and repeat for clarity.

- Think about the words you use towards each other—do they inspire, motivate, and/ or encourage?

Reminders to Self

Physical touch is another wa
to show genuine affection.

Gifts coming from the heart that are
personalised, meaningful, keepsakes, or
memorable items show thoughtfulness and care.

Some people need to hear how you feel about them
to reaffirm the relationship and establish a deeper
connection.

There are many ways to show love.

Quality time, spending time with those you love,
is one way to demonstrate your love.

Acts of service, doing something for another person
in need, is a great way to demonstrate your love.

Physical touch is another way to show
genuine affection.

Reflections

Question Time: Love language exercise

What quality time ideas do you have? Be creative!

What physical touch ideas do you have? No inhibitions.

What words of affirmation ideas do you have? Express yourself

---

What acts of service ideas do you have? Be thoughtful.

What gifting ideas do you have? Give from the heart.

Faye Thompson

Words of Affirmation

Look in the mirror and repeat with conviction:

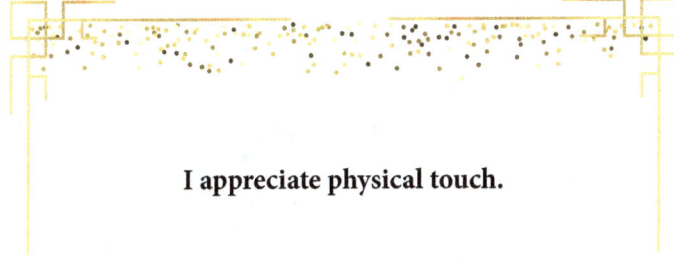

I appreciate physical touch.

I can do acts of meaningful service.

I give with a loving heart.

I speak from a place of love.

I value quality time.

Time for Tips!

Let's get thinking

The do's and the don'ts: things that can ruin relationships if not handled carefully or thoughtfully.

The Don'ts

- X Abuse of any kind.
- X Avoidance.
- X Acting like roommates, which can lead to bickering, backbiting, or battling.
- X Coldness or non-affection.
- X Constant arguments.
- X Detrimental secrets.
- X Dominating.
- X Forgetting special occasions.

- ✕ Fighting over money issues (educate yourselves on wealth-building principles).

- ✕ Imbalance: who's doing all the giving/taking all the time?

- ✕ A lack of appreciation.

- ✕ A lack of encouragement.

- ✕ A lack of intimacy.

- ✕ A lack of joy.

- ✕ A lack of kindness.

- ✕ A lack of trust.

- ✕ Non-constructive criticism.

- ✕ Physical neglect.

- ✕ Possessiveness, tight-fistedness envy, and greed.

- ✕ Trying to keep something that no longer serves you.

The Do's: the healthier way forward

- ✓ Tip #1: Do the opposite of the don'ts!
- ✓ Amazing intimacy: know what you both enjoy, without inhibitions/reservations/hang-ups or self-consciousness.
- ✓ Be proud of each other and your achievements.
- ✓ Listening to each other with an open mind.
- ✓ Encourage each other.
- ✓ Enjoy an active life together.
- ✓ Express your gratefulness.
- ✓ Find ways to feel closer to your partner without stifling him/her.
- ✓ Be friends first.
- ✓ Get some 'me' time.
- ✓ Give each other positive suggestions as to how to improve each other's lives.
- ✓ Have things in common, including a mutual friendship circle.
- ✓ Help each other; lift some of the burdens.
- ✓ Hold hands.

The Do's: the healthier way forward

- ✓ Hug/cuddle like you mean it.
- ✓ Being okay doing things together and apart.
- ✓ Kiss like you mean it!
- ✓ Mutual appreciation.
- ✓ Mutual respect.
- ✓ Recognition that the relationship has raised your standards and status.
- ✓ Replenish yourself so you can give appreciation.
- ✓ Take pleasure in giving pleasure with/to each other; no motives, just love.
- ✓ Be present in the time you have together.
- ✓ Thoughtfulness.
- ✓ Warm affection.
- ✓ Ask what you can do to help maintain and progress the relationship.
- ✓ If your partner is a major challenge in your life, his/her purpose is to help you grow.

Be kinder, compassionate, and considerate

Overall, I feel that we would have a much better world and be in much better positions if we all could be kinder, more compassionate, and more considerate humans.

Perhaps, we could take a few leaves from the African love birds' trees—they show affection and spend time bonding with each other, they mate for life, and at times, live in a mutual social circle. Unfortunately, though, they don't like chocolate, which wouldn't work for me!

My point is that we can't just wait for Valentine's Day to express our love for someone in a way both people in a relationship find pleasing. You should come home to love and not a living nightmare.

At some point in our lives, we require various levels of support from our significant others. It's not that we lean on them as much as we sap their energies and have major expectations.

Toxic co-dependency

Co-dependency can become toxic if you are unable to cope without someone constantly validating your worth or needing him to be your source of wellbeing. What happens if he goes away on business, or is ill and can no longer help you due to incapacity? Co-dependency shows up in things like reacting instead of responding, controlling behaviour, low self-esteem with your partner/spouse, blame, harmful or unproductive communication, and manipulative behaviour.

Do you swim or sink into the inability to cope because you rely on your partner too much?

With the right knowledge, it is possible for you to be an interdependent couple. This is when a couple can do activities apart and together, and neither one leans too heavily on the other. You have mutual friends and your own friends; you are able to respect each other and go out either together or apart. This means that you value the other person and you remain distinct individuals; however, it also means that you're able to show your openness and vulnerability to your partner, you can still have emotional intimacy, and you still have a sense of yourself.

This allows you and your partner to be yourselves. This is not a compromise, but the way you show that you value each other as unique people.

If you're too dependent on your partner, it may lead to an unhealthy relationship with everything placed on the need of the other person for continual support. When you are too dependent, you can become a burden to your partner, and if you find life a heavy load to bear, your inability to know where you end and your partner begins is bound to cause some issues. The inability to take any responsibility for yourself or your actions and the tendency to leave it all to the other person can be perceived as one-sided and selfish.

Ask yourself the question: what happens when the help is gone? Will you be surprised? Will you understand the part you played in totally draining your partner's essence? Are you a person who spends their life saying it's unreasonable and you can't cope because your partner doesn't carry out your every wish?

This can develop worry and anxiety for yourself, and you will not be on the road to a growth mindset.

A caution on independence

On the other side, independence is useful and advantageous, but not if it is taken to the extreme. If you show that you can do it all by yourself all the time, you may find that your partner thinks they are not needed, and you will be unable to make a connection emotionally or intimately with them in a way that is meaningful. This may also be interpreted that you do not value your relationship.

As unique humans, we have different ways of expressing love with the people with whom we pair. Both of you may find you're the perfect match, while at other times, we do not, and you may decide to move on to someone else. Whatever you do, be sure to make yourself happy first to create a balanced life for yourself. Remember to make yourself happy, simply because it shouldn't lie exclusively in the hands of your partner or spouse.

On our journeys through life, we all go through transformations and transitions, and along the way, some people will stay with or around us to the end of days, some people will go, and some of them will return. Everything in your life is for a reason, a season, a lesson, or a blessing.

Start with a friendship

At the end of the day, we all change—it's inevitable—but the question is: can you maintain a friendship with your partner first?

If you dated or even married someone because of their looks but you realised they have a compromising attitude, or if you dated someone for material gain, maybe you noticed down the line that they have poor family values—what happens when the looks have gone? With what will you be left?

Let me be real: it's not every day that we look like our best, scrubbed-up versions; true? The way you look on the weekends when you're out with friends and family is after you've had the time to brush up. Take a look at the same person in the morning, their daily work-look, wearing old specs and with dishevelled hair after a hard day—can you and do you still love their spirit and personality? This is a test of the heart!

Real life has no filters

Nowadays, we only post the best filtered photos on social media, but people need to see you both polished and unpolished.

It's clear to me that people like it when you look decent, tidy, and well-kept, but this is not always the reality of everyday life. People need to contemplate that we have the same hearts with glasses on as when wearing contact lenses and a bit of makeup or a smart shirt.

Sure, we all can look like the cat's whiskers on a night out, but will you still love your significant other when they are sick and in need of help? Could you be the person who cleans your loved one up when they can no longer manage for themselves, or at least find an appropriate caregiver for them?

Growing old with your partner?

While we are on the subject, if someone doesn't like you for your inner-being, you will find it really challenging to grow old age with that person in a loving and fulfilling way.

God willing, we all hope to live into our senior years. We all eventually lose our tight, collagen-endowed skin, our hair textures change, the colour will fade to platinum or silver, our body parts will wear down and not work as well, and our flesh may lose shape and go south. However, the ultimate question is: will you still love and care about your significant other because, in your eyes, they have an amazing spirit?

By the way, just because we get older, there's no reason not to keep up with the gentle exercise, stay fit, and have a healthy diet; continue honouring your temple.

Most importantly, be yourself. If you know there's a part of you that's not so great, find ways to develop personally or educate yourself.

In this life, we have a lot for which to be grateful, and when you have caring, considerate, and compassionate people in your life, it makes it so much greater.

Reminders to Self

Be kind, compassionate, and considerate.

Strive to be mutually independent, do activities apart and together, and try not to lean too heavily on each other.

Your happiness shouldn't depend upon your partner or spouse.

Take care of yourself as you get older: honour your temple, educate yourself, surround yourself with caring, considerate, and compassionate people.

Take the time to be thankful every day.

Send love, kindness, care, and compassion.

Reflections

Question Time: The do's and don'ts

List three (3) don'ts of which you have been guilty in your past relationships.

1. _____

2. _____

3. _____

What were the consequences for that/those relationships?

_____

List three (3) do's you practise to set your relationships up for success.

1. _____

2. _____

3. _____

Words of Affirmation

Look in the mirror and repeat with conviction:

I am a priority.

I am compassionate.

I am considerate.

I am generous.

I am hilarious.

I am intelligent.

I am joyful.

I am kind.

I am living my best life.

I am outstanding.

I am special.

I am strong.

I am talented.

I am unique.

I am vibrant.

I am who I am.

Glossary of Words and Terms

Affirmation: the action or process of declaring something to be true; something emotional, supporting, or encouraging.

Commitment: dedicated to something or someone; devotion and loyalty.

Communication: the ability to get information across to someone, typically through words but also through gestures and body language. Persistence and patience maintain positive communication.

Forgiveness: the act of pardoning someone from their transgressions against you and letting go of the pain and burden of a bad memory or action.

Freedom: to be free without physical restraint or mental confinement.

Gratitude: being thankful; the ability to show appreciation.

Happiness: the feeling of being happy from the inside; the feeling of contentment and satisfaction within.

Honesty: telling the truth.

Intimacy: noun—close familiarity or friendship ('Oxford Dictionary'). Euphemistic—sexual intercourse.

Love:
noun—an intense feeling of deep affection;
verb—to feel deep affection or sexual love for someone. There are typically four types of love:
eros—erotic, passionate love;
philia—love of friends and equals;
storge—love for parents and for children; and
agape—love of mankind.

Positive: constructive, optimistic, or confident.

Positive communication: to share feelings in a considerate way.

Reliability: being consistently trustworthy; sticking to the agreement or plan.

Resolve conflicts: to find a solution for a problem or issue.

Respect: noun—a feeling of deep admiration for someone or something elicited by the abilities, qualities, or achievements he/it possesses.

Self: the set of someone's characteristics—such as personality and ability—that are not physical and make that person different from other people (Cambridge Dictionary).

Support: to hold someone up or have his back; to carry the weight; to underpin or reinforce the help needed to keep things running smoothly.

Trust: confidently believing in someone or something without a shadow of doubt.

A-Z of Positive Words

Amazing	Nurturing
Big-hearted	Optimistic
Considerate	Passionate
Deserving	Queenly
Empathetic	Quality
Friendly	Romantic
Gorgeous	Successful
Hospitable	Talented
Imaginative	Uplifting
Jovial	Veracious
Kind	Worthy
King	Xenial
Liberated	YOLO
Mindful	Zealous

About the Author

Faye Thompson, born and raised in south London, is a 47-year-old mother of two beautiful and talented children. She is a qualified reiki and crystal reiki practitioner, holds a diploma in Homeopathy and is also a Montessori trained directress with an international teaching diploma.

She is the eldest child of three and has a proud and wonderful heritage as a woman of colour. Her father is from Kilmarnock, St Elizabeth, on the sunny island of Jamaica, and her mother is British from Croydon, with family links to Dry Drayton, Cambridge.

She has been in the childcare care industry for more than 30 years as a private nanny and in private day care. She holds an NNEB diploma and a Montessori international teaching diploma as well as qualifications in Leadership and Management. In her career, she has attended an array of courses related to childcare and education.

Faye has reignited her passion for baking Jamaican patties and a variety of cakes, inspired by her late grandmothers Edna and Sylvia.

Acknowledgements

My journey to writing my book began when I attended the Conscious Dreams Publishing 'Power of Your Story' two-day workshop. During the workshop, I was given a challenge to find five family or friends that would support me on that journey. I'm blessed to say that I have many!

So much love and respect to my originals. My foundation supporters. My darling daughter Nika, my not-so-little sister Selena, my friends Susana M, Sayyara and my bonafide bredrin Henry. They've supported me from the beginning with words of encouragement, advice or offered to support me in whatever way they could from start to end.

Also, Jackie S, who was on the workshop with me. Thank you for your contribution. What a powerful workshop group we had over those two days.

I thank the people who raised funds in a small secret crowdfunding project. Thank you to community leader Donna M-T and Ishia who always checked in on me, ready in prayer when I was going through 'stuff'.

Thank you to the Waterstones ladies Joanna.B, Karen H and Jenessa Q for being constant cheerleaders.

To all my aunties, uncles and cousins that have wished me well or contributed through crowdfunding...especially Aunty Karen, Aunty Jacqui, my cousins Yvie and Melissa. I thank you wholeheartedly!

To all my friends from back in the day, who believed in me especially gratitude to my old bestie Lorraine A-S. Also, Carril, we go back a long way to when our firstborns were babies. I am grateful to you Sistar!

To Joan, for contributing towards my book, also for being a woman of wisdom, encouragement, jokes and who is a little partial to my cakes and patties. Ever grateful.

To Caron, who saw that I had a dream of writing a book and wanted to help me make that dream become a reality. Thank you, you have!

To my dearest friend Annette H, big sister from another mother! Thank you for all your support and love in the past and for contributing towards my book in this present time.

Thank you, Jo.L and family.

Thank you, Annika.C, my reiki friend.

To the people I've not even met, and you still supported the cause Afrah T, Kim F, Rick.T, Sergey.K and to all the anonymous pledgers thank you so much x

Thank you to one of my editors, Elise Abrams.

Thank you Ces Rosanna Price for the beautiful book design and thank you Amit Dey for typesetting.

Now, last but most certainly not least, in fact there's no way I could have taken this journey without my Book Journey Mentor and editor. The awesome and amazing Daniella Blechner from Conscious Dreams Publishing. She has worked tirelessly on the entire process and supported me the whole way …nudging whilst I was procrastinating and encouraging me. Thank you for being a lovely, genuine dear friend and soul sister Danni B. Thank you so, so much. xxx

Special Dedication

I'd like to take a moment to offer a sincere and wholehearted thank you for all those who contributed towards my crowdfunding campaign so that I could make my dream on my vision board to publish my own book possible. I couldn't have done it without your support!

From my heart to yours, thank you to:
Nika T, Danni B, Henry B, Aunty Karen N, Aunty Jacqui J, Yvie C, Melissa M, Karen H. Joanna B, Lorraine A-S, Susana M, Donna M-T, Ishia B, Joan N, Annika C, Caron L, Jo L, Kim F, Jackie S, Carill A, Afrah T, Rick T, Sergey K

And to all the anonymous pledgers and silent supporters – you know who you are xx

Conscious Dreams
PUBLISHING

Transforming diverse writers
into successful published authors

www.consciousdreamspublishing.com

authors@consciousdreamspublishing.com

Let's connect

www.ingramcontent.com/pod-product-compliance
Lightning Source LLC
Chambersburg PA
CBHW050417120526
44590CB00015B/1995